GRAND CANY

What goes down must come up

EXPLORE THE GREAT GC

LISA JEWEL
&
Bookswithsoul.com

For Nancy,
Thank you for your everlasting friendship. We've
walked, hiked, ran and crawled our way through many
tight spots together. I may never have discovered all
the wonderful trails within the boundaries of Arizona
without you!

Thank you for being my hiking partner

Co-writer & Contributor Anita Kaltenbaugh
Cover Photo by Lisa Rafferty
What goes down must come up
Explore the Great GC — Grand Canyon Hiking Journal
Thanks to cover model Coleen Martin.
Check out all our titles on amazon.com/author/bookswithsoul

THIS HIKING JOURNAL BELONGS TO:

HIKE ON

YOUR BIG ADVENTURE AWAITS
IT'S TIME!

IT'S TIME TO CHALLENGE
YOUR INNER CORE AND HIKE
ONE OF THE SEVEN WONDERS
OF THE WORLD.

IT'S TIME TO TRAIN YOUR
BODY AND BE PREPARED.
IT'S TIME TO
ORGANIZE AND PLAN
YOUR TRIP,

IT'S TIME TO CAPTURE
REFLECTIONS OF YOUR
PHENOMENAL ADVENTURE.

IT'S TIME TO RECORD YOUR
MEMORIES.
SET A GOAL, MAKE A PLAN.

GRAND CANYON HIKING JOURNAL,
"WHAT GOES DOWN, MUST COME UP"
WILL HELP YOU ACCOMPLISH YOUR
GOALS AND RECORD AN ADVENTURE OF
A LIFETIME.

Table of contents

Section 1
Fun facts about the Grand Canyon

Section 2
Checklist: The Essentials for your Day Hike
Tips for great day hiking in the Canyon
Hazards: Be prepared for anything

Section 3
Recommended Hikes
where to sleep

Section 4
Journal Pages & Moments of Reflections

Section 5
Maps
FAQ

It's time to record your memories.

SECTION ONE
FUN FACTS ABOUT THE GRAND CANYON

WHAT GOES DOWN, MUST COME UP
EXPLORE THE GREAT GC - GRAND CANYON
HIKING JOURNAL

SECTION ONE
FUN FACTS ABOUT THE GRAND CANYON

"OF ALL THE PATHS YOU MAKE IN LIFE, MAKE SURE A FEW OF THEM ARE DIRT"

JOHN MUIR

Fun Facts About the Grand Canyon (GC)

- The GC is 277 miles in length within the protected boundaries of the national park, that exceeds 1.2 million acres. Nearly all of the backcountry has retained much of its primeval character.

- The GC is not just one canyon but a canyon system; a canyon within a canyon, carved by the mighty Colorado river.

- The GC is one of the world's greatest natural wonders!

- At its widest point the Grand Canyon stretches 18 miles across.

- The GC is carved by the copper-colored Colorado River, the rock layers record billions of years of history.

- The GC was discovered in 1540 by a group of Europeans in their quest to find the Seven Cities of Gold.

FUN FACTS ABOUT THE GRAND CANYON

- Supai Village, the capital of the Havasupai Indian Reservation, boasts a population of several hundred residents living inside the Grand Canyon.

- The Village holds the record for the most remote city in the continental United States.

- There is a U.S. postal office at Phantom Ranch. Mail service still travels by mule today.

- Commercial flights over the GC ended in the late 1950's after a tragic mid-air accident where two planes collided, killing 128 people.

- John Wesley Powell was the first white man to see the Grand Canyon in 1869 (after the civil war).

- The Grand Canyon is 7,000 ft above sea level at its highest point.

- The North Rim is 1,000 ft higher in elevation than the South Rim. Due to colder temperatures, the North Rim is closed mid-October to mid-May.

DID YOU KNOW:

The desert can be extremely hot or cold when lightning strikes. It can reach up to 30,000 degrees Celsius (54,000 degrees Fahrenheit).

The Grand Canyon National Park is bigger than the entire State of Rhode Island.

There are hidden caves in the Canyon. Even though over 1,000 caves are said to exist, only 335 are reported.

Only one cave is open to the public, the **Cave of the Domes** on Horseshoe Mesa.

The Grand Canyon has a conspiracy theory attached to its history. In the early 1900's the *Arizona Gazette* reported an ancient civilization lived in the tunnels of the Grand Canyon. The Smithsonian stated it was a hoax, others believe it is a government cover-up.

Did you know:

Many tourists show up to the Grand Canyon unprepared. They decide to take a beautiful hike, and when they get down in the canyon, they find they have difficulty getting back up. Always remember, **what goes down must come up**. Be prepared.

Think pink. The Grand Canyon is home to rare pink rattlesnakes, which blend into the surrounding rocks.

If you are seeking clean air, this is your spot. The Grand Canyon boasts being a participant of the "Cleanest Air in the United States Club".

According to the National Park Services, the Grand Canyon is missing nearly 950 million years of rock.

Where did it go? The canyon is part of a phenomenon known as the Great Unconformity. The mystery, 250 million old rock layers are against 1.2 billion-year rocks. How did this happen?

"ADVENTURES FEED YOUR SOUL"

SECTION TWO

CHECKLIST: THE ESSENTIALS FOR YOUR DAY HIKE

TIPS FOR GREAT DAY HIKING IN THE CANYON
HAZARDS: BE PREPARED FOR ANYTHING

SECTION TWO

CHECKLIST: THE ESSENTIALS FOR YOUR DAY HIKE

TIPS FOR GREAT DAY HIKING IN THE CANYON
HAZARDS: BE PREPARED FOR ANYTHING

Checklist:
The Essentials for your Day Hike

- **Check the weather conditions**: Watch for flash floods; check trail maps, study maps for escape routes and move to higher ground immediately if you hear or see a flash flood.

- **Clothing**: Remember to pack for the cool desert nights. Wear loose comfortable clothes. Consider wearing a light-colored long sleeve shirt. Women – wear a sports bra, you'll thank me later. Take your T-shirt off to soak in the water at the river, stream or water stations.

- **Water:** Don't skimp – pack at least 1 gallon of water per person per day. Drink half to a full liter per hour of hiking. Check out trails for water availability (water availability is seasonal). Bring along refillable water bottles or a hydration backpack.

Sunscreen: You're not here for the tan; leave the SPF 8 at home. Consider bringing SPF 30 or higher in the desert, especially if you'll be sweating and hiking for prolonged periods.

- **Shoes:** Even if you are not an experienced hiker, having comfortable shoes with good tread will be important. Don't wear your brand-new hiking shoes for the first time in the GC. Have your shoes properly broken-in, to avoid blisters. Adjust the laces for hiking down the trails, versus going up the trail. Make sure you have room for your toes as you hike down.

- **Hat & Sunglasses:** The sun is intense, and shade is limited. You need a hat and sunglasses. Bring a bandana to help stay cool, wet it down if necessary.

- **Moleskin & second pair of socks:** Well worn shoes are your friends to keep your feet happy. Sweaty feet combined with the canyon's steep trails are a recipe for blisters and hot spots. At the first sign of a rub or hot spot, remove your shoes and air-dry your feet, apply moleskin, tape or band-aids as needed.

Checklist

- [ ] _____
- [ ] _____
- [ ] _____
- [ ] _____
- [ ] _____
- [ ] _____
- [ ] _____
- [ ] _____
- [ ] _____
- [ ] _____
- [ ] _____
- [ ] _____
- [ ] _____
- [ ] _____
- [ ] _____
- [ ] _____
- [ ] _____
- [ ] _____
- [ ] _____

- **Food:** Pack high energy snacks, sufficient proteins and fats such as cheese, crackers, PBJ sandwiches, dried meats. Consider bringing salty snacks to avoid or treat muscle cramps. Your cooler will heat up in a sun-drenched car, be careful what you leave behind.

- **Map:** Bring a detailed map of your hike and even a general road atlas will guide you along the highways; you can't count on getting a mobile signal in the backcountry.

- **Flashlight:** Depending on the time of year, waiting for the shade may cause you to hike out in the near dark. Also a blacklight flashlight to see scorpions if hiking at night or camping might be useful.

- **Camera:** You'll want to remember this trip, bring extra batteries or charger for your phone. There is limited service at the bottom of the canyon. Tip: A solar charger would be great.

Checklist

- [ ] _____
- [ ] _____
- [ ] _____
- [ ] _____
- [ ] _____
- [ ] _____
- [ ] _____
- [ ] _____
- [ ] _____
- [ ] _____
- [ ] _____
- [ ] _____
- [ ] _____
- [ ] _____
- [ ] _____
- [ ] _____
- [ ] _____
- [ ] _____
- [ ] _____
- [ ] _____

Tips for great day-hiking in the Canyon

- **Be kind to yourself**: Don't exceed your normal activity level. If you have medical problems such as bad knees, bad back, heart problems or asthma, remember hiking in the canyon combined with the intense heat, will make these conditions worse.

- **Let the shade hit the trail before you do**: Consider waiting for the shade to hike uphill. You will use more energy hiking in the full sun while trying to stay cool, then hiking in the shade.

- **Plan for additional time to walk out of the canyon**: It will take you at least double the amount of time to walk up and out of the canyon than to go down. Be prepared for warmer temperatures as you descend into the canyon.

- **Create your own Evap System:** Stay wet, stay cool; when you are near water, take off your shirt, soak your shirt, allowing yourself to cool down. This will help you stay refreshed throughout the day.

- **Don't forget to eat and avoid water intoxication:** Your body uses enormous amounts of energy to keep you cool in the heat, so eat up. This is your best defense from water intoxication and exhaustion. Heat reduces your appetite and you'll be craving water. Keep your water bottle handy, sip the water and eat small amounts of food throughout the hike. Your Grand Canyon hike isn't your diet plan!

Checklist

- ☐ _____
- ☐ _____
- ☐ _____
- ☐ _____
- ☐ _____
- ☐ _____
- ☐ _____
- ☐ _____
- ☐ _____
- ☐ _____
- ☐ _____
- ☐ _____
- ☐ _____
- ☐ _____
- ☐ _____
- ☐ _____
- ☐ _____
- ☐ _____
- ☐ _____

"IT IS NOT THE MOUNTAIN WE CONQUER, BUT OURSELVES"

SIR EDMUND HILLARY

HAZARDS: BE PREPARED FOR ANYTHING

- **Heat:** This is a real threat in the Grand Canyon, and you need to consider the time of your hike for safe hiking. Temperatures increase as you descend into the canyon. The walk up and out of the canyon is more physically demanding than going down.
  - Heat Stroke and Heat Exhaustion are potential hazards.

- **Dehydration:** The Arizona desert air is so dry that you may not realize you are sweating, as the sweat quickly evaporates. Drink plenty of water. Signs of dehydration: dry mouth, headaches, sleepiness, extreme thirst, dry skin and decreased urine output.

- **Animals:** Rock squirrel is the most dangerous animal in the GC. Most trips to the urgent care are due to bites from this ferocious, innocent looking creature. Don't feed the squirrels.
  - Other animals: Coyote, bat, squirrel, raccoon, bobcat, gray fox, mountain lion, elk.
  - Approximately 90 mammal species call the GC home.
  - Many insects, snakes and lizards call the GC home. Be alert of your surroundings both in the day-time and at night.

- **Flash Floods**: Heavy rainfall, even miles away can cause flash flooding, sending huge amounts of water down dry washes, transforming these dry wash beds into raging rivers. Move to higher ground immediately if you hear or see a flash flood.

- **Lightning:** On average it strikes 25,000 times per year in the GC. Monsoon season brings thunderstorms and lightning in Arizona from July to September. While beautiful to see, you need to be aware of the danger. Be aware of the nearest safe structure or vehicle.

- **Learn where the emergency phones are located on the trails:**
  - Take cover if you find yourself in an approaching thunderstorm or storm system.
  - If your hair stands on end, a strike is looming. RUN.
  - Move away from the edge, avoid rocky outcrops, lone trees, poles, and railings.
  - Look for safe structure, not your tent.
  - If there is no shelter; spread out from other people.
  - Crouch on the balls of your feet with your heels touching, head down and hands covering ears. Do not touch the ground. Do not lie flat on the ground.

WHAT GOES DOWN, MUST COME UP
EXPLORE THE GREAT GC – GRAND CANYON
HIKING JOURNAL

SECTION THREE
RECOMMENDED
HIKES
WHERE TO SLEEP

WHAT GOES DOWN, MUST COME UP
EXPLORE THE GREAT GC – GRAND CANYON
HIKING JOURNAL

SECTION THREE

RECOMMENDED
HIKES
WHERE TO SLEEP

"WONDER, WANDER, REPEAT"

Recommended Hikes

- **Hermit Trail to Dripping Springs Day Hike** (Easy to moderate; 6.5 miles roundtrip)
  - 1500 feet elevation change
  - Drive to the trailhead if the shuttle is not running (March 1st to Nov 30th)
  - Not frequently traveled
  - Look for fossil footprints in the Coconino sandstone on the switchbacks
  - Follow Hermit Trail for 1.5 miles, then junction to Dripping Springs Trail (turn left) passing Boucher Trail, until you reach the springs in .5 miles

- **Grandview Trail to Horseshoe Mesa Day Hike** (Moderate; 6.5 miles round-trip)
  - 3,000 feet elevation change
  - Hike is very steep in the beginning
  - Fill up water at the top, as the next source of water is at the bottom (Page Spring)

Recommended Hikes

- **South Kaibab/Tonto/Bright Angel Day Hike**
  (Strenuous; 13-mile loop)
    - Start on South Kaibab; there is no water on this part of the trail.
    - This hike offers glorious views of the inner gorge, temples and buttes.
    - Bright Angel from Indian Gardens offers water seasonally, as well as every mile and a half as you hike up.
    - Take note, this is a steep hike due to a quick elevation gain of 3000 feet as you hike back to the rim. You'll share portions of this trail with hikers and mule/pack stock.

- **Horseshoe Mesa Backpack**
  (Moderate; 12-mile loop)
    - Fill up with water at Grandview Point parking lot; your next source of water is 3.75 miles into your hike. You will descend into the canyon with an elevation change of 3,000 feet.
    - A side trail to Cave of Domes is accessible from this hike. It is the only GC cave that doesn't require a special permit to enter.
    - The final leg of the hike has an elevation gain of more than 3,500 feet, as you climb from Cottonwood Creek to the Grandview Trail, continuing all the way to the rim.
    - Planning on camping? Call Backcountry Information Center (928-638-7875) to check on Cottonwood Creek (creek runs seasonally).

"THE BEST VIEW COMES AFTER THE HARDEST CLIMB."

RECOMMENDED HIKES

- **Rim Trail Day Hike**
  (Easy-shaded; 13-mile)
    - Mostly asphalt, mainly a flat trail along the canyon's South Rim.
    - Portions of the trail are wheelchair accessible from Monument Creek Vista to Hermits Rest.
    - The South Rim Trail is a largely flat paved trail that begins at Grand Canyon Village or along Hermit Road.
    - You'll have the ability to pick up different sections of the Rim Trail and select how much time and distance you want to cover. You'll also be able to view over 1,700 plant species and hopefully encounter one of the local animal species that call the Grand Canyon home.
    - Shuttle Bus service allows you to hike in one direction and return by bus. Shuttle bus to Hermits Rest Route operates from March 1 to November 30. Return trip has limited stops at Hermits Rest, Pima, Mohave and Powell Points.
    - As you move East from South Kaibab to Trailview Overlook (approximately 7 miles) you'll have the opportunity to view the Canyon from many different angles; across, up and down the Canyon.
    - Hopi Point is a great spot to take in the sunset and Colorado river views.
    - Grandview Point provides the most stunning and grand views of the Grand Canyon. This vantage point provides you with your first glimpse of a tiny stretch of the Colorado River miles away.
    - Continue your walk to "The Abyss" (3.4 miles) viewing area, with a vertical drop of over 3,000 feet. You'll see the Tonto Plateau as well as the Colorado River, far below.
    - Pima Point allows you to hear the Colorado River and provides stunning sunrise and sunset views.
    - Hermits Rest provides canyon views, drinking water, restrooms and picnic tables.

- **Bright Angel Trail to Plateau Point**
  (Moderate- Well-Maintained; 12-mile)
    - 12 miles roundtrip with 3,000 feet of elevation change (up and down)
    - The Bright Angel trail is well groomed and a great trail for families and people doing their first hike into the deep Canyon. It offers amazing views, water and bathrooms along the way.
    - Be prepared for an all-day adventure. The trail has long gradual switch-backs that descend toward a more level trail as you approach Indian Gardens about 4.5 miles down. You'll find shade, water and bathrooms here as well.
    - The trail to Plateau Point is to the west of Indian Gardens. This trail has a rolling flat trail, that is well groomed approximately a 1.5-mile hike to the edge of the Tonto Plateau.
    - You'll view the roaring Colorado River from this vantage point. It is one of the spectacular view of the canyon, the inner gorge and the canyon that lays beyond your reach on the North side.
    - Allow enough time for your return trip up Bright Angel Trail which is a long arduous hike, typically taking twice as long to hike those last 4.5 miles of switchback from Indian Gardens to the top of the South Rim as it did going down.

- **South Kaibab Trail to Ooh Aah Point to Cedar Ridge**
  (Easy-Moderate - 9/10 of a mile)
    - While this hike is not long in distance, the trail is made up of steps, not a smooth flat path. Note, in some areas the steps are deeply gorged due to the mule traffic.
    - This very short hike approximately 9/10 of a mile, brings you to a beautiful spot to view the Canyon in all of its glory. The Ooh Aah Point is at the corner of a tight switchback with giant rocks that give you a taste of the sheer drop off within the Canyon walls. This is a great photo spot.
    - Extend to Cedar Ridge approximately .5 mile past Ooh Aah Point for a bathroom. There is no water on South Kaibab.
    - Rest here, take a drink of water and a quick snack before heading back up the tight switchback step trail to the top.
    - Remember, what goes down, must come up… your way to the top is much more difficult than the way down.

"LEAVE THE ROAD, TAKE THE TRAILS"

WHERE TO SLEEP:

Grand Canyon National Park Lodging:

El Tovar, Phantom Ranch, Maswik Lodge, Thunderbird Lodge, Kachina Lodge, Bright Angel Lodge & Cabins and The Grand Hotel.

- Read all about each individual & unique property at https://www.grandcanyonlodges.com/lodging/
- Call 888-29-PARKS

Phantom Ranch: inside the canyon

- Call 888-29-PARKS
- If you want to be in the canyon, plan far, far, far (at least a year) ahead and try to secure a coveted reservation below the rim at Phantom Ranch. Only way to get there is to hike, ride a mule or on a whitewater rafting trip. Basic accommodations… but a once in a lifetime experience.

El Tovar Hotel: on the rim

- (888) 297-2757 Grand Canyon Village, AZ 86023
- Historic landmark dating back to 1905 and perched on the rim of the canyon.
- A 14-minute walk from Grand Canyon Village and an 8-minute walk from Grand Canyon Railway.

Kachina: on the rim

- (888) 297-2757 Grand Canyon Village, AZ 86023
- Sits on the edge of the canyon, many rooms have partial views. For hikers it is fantastic It is directly on the Rim Trail and is in the middle of the historic district. Hike the Rim Trail from Hermits Rest to the Kaibab Trailhead, approximately 12.8 miles. Secret tip: partial canyon views available, called canyon-side rooms.

Maswik Lodge:

- (888) 297-2757 Grand Canyon Village, AZ 86023
- Comfortable rooms only ¼ mile from the rim. Pizza pub, gift shop and in the pines.

Thunderbird Lodge:

- (888) 297-2757 Grand Canyon Village, AZ 86023
- Family-focused lodging in the heart of the historic village. Short walk to the Bright Angel Trail Head, restaurants and gift shops.

Bright Angel Lodge and Cabins:

- 888-29-PARKS Grand Canyon Village, AZ 86023
- History abounds in this area of cabins and lodge. Secret tip: There are two specialty historic cabins that can only be reserved by phone but worth the wait and effort. Buckey O'Neill Cabin and Red Horse Cabin.

The Grand Hotel at the Grand Canyon

- (928) 638-3333 Grand Canyon Village, AZ 86023
- Part of the Grand Canyon National Park lodging. A contemporary style hotel offering a restaurant, saloon and indoor pool. Two miles from the Grand Canyon Park.

Grand Canyon Railway & Hotel:

- (928) 635-4010 235 N Grand Canyon Blvd, Williams, AZ 86046
- Stay In Williams, AZ, explore the town and take the memorable Grand Canyon Railway to the canyon and back to the Williams.

ALSO: CHECK WWW.AIRBNB.COM FOR AIRBNB OPTIONS

Camping:

Under Canvas Grand Canyon

- https://www.undercanvas.com/camps/grand-canyon/
- Glamping experience like no other. A night under a million stars. Spend the day at the South Rim hiking, then travel 30 miles to another priceless adventure. End your adventures in the pines and junipers under the stars, camping with style.

National Park Services (NPS) campgrounds within Grand Canyon National Park.

- **Mather Campground** on the South Rim, located in Grand Canyon Village, Open All Year

- **Desert View Campground** is a first-come/first - served basis, located 25 miles (41 km) to the east of Grand Canyon Village.

- **Bright Angel Campground-** Hike down Bright Angel Trail (10 miles down) and secure a campsite. Secret tip is to be near the water. They do have flushing toilets, and a walk over to Phantom Ranch will score you a few necessities.

North Rim

- **North Rim-** located in Utah only 10% of visitors visit the North Rim due to its higher elevation of more than 8,000, and its seasonal restrictions.

- **Grand Canyon Lodge** - **North Rim -**Rustic cabin lodge in the pines. If you are a nature lover and willing to take a longer trek, grab peace and solitude in the cooler rim. A historic treasure deep in the trees and along the canyon edge.

- **North Rim Campground** - Open May 15 through October 31.

- **North Rim** is very different than the popular South Rim. If you decide to do a rim-to-rim you will be hiking approximately 26 miles through the canyon to the South Rim. The first 4 miles down is steep and wooded.

"ALL GOOD THINGS ARE WILD AND FREE"

Yavapai Lodge and Trailer Village RV Park

- 2-star hotel
- (877) 404-4611 Grand Canyon Village, AZ 86023
- Basic rooms, pet friendly, mini-fridge. Walk one mile to South Rim.

Best Western Premier Grand Canyon Squire Inn

- 4-star hotel
- (928) 638-2681 Grand Canyon Village, AZ 86023
- A modern hotel with pool, restaurants and lounge. This hotel is 7.5 miles from Grand Canyon National Park.

Grand Canyon Plaza Hotel

- 3-star hotel
- (928) 638-2673 Grand Canyon Village, AZ 86023
- Comfortable rooms that offer a free shuttle, buffet restaurant and indoor and outdoor hot tubs.

Red Feather Lodge (author's pick, clean & inexpensive)

- 2-star hotel
- (928) 638-2414 Grand Canyon Village, AZ 86023
- Basic but comfortable, with outdoor pool and shuttle. One mile from the South Rim not the canyons edge.

Holiday Inn Express Grand Canyon

- 3-star hotel
- (928) 638- 3000 Grand Canyon Village, AZ 86023
- Short drive from the canyon and comfortable rooms. Watch the sunset and come back for the free breakfast buffet.

SECTION FOUR

JOURNAL PAGES MOMENTS OF REFLECTIONS

SECTION FOUR

JOURNAL PAGES
MOMENTS OF
REFLECTIONS

"THE EARTH HAS MUSIC FOR THOSE WHO LISTEN"

Shakespeare

THE HIKE

TRAIL NAME:
LENGTH OF TRAIL, LEVEL OF DIFFICULTY, AVERAGE HIKING TIME:

FEATURES OF THE HIKE:
HIKING PARTNERS, ELEVATION CHANGES, WATER AVAILABILITY
(WATER CACHE AREAS) :

MOMENTS OF REFLECTION:
WHAT I MOST WANT TO REMEMBER ABOUT THIS HIKE, SCENIC
VIEWPOINTS:

DATE:

_____

_____

_____

_____

_____

_____

_____

_____

_____

_____

_____

_____

_____

TAKE A DEEP BREATH, TILT YOUR HEAD BACK— WRITE WHAT'S ON YOUR
MIND...

DATE:

_____

_____

_____

_____

_____

_____

_____

_____

_____

_____

_____

_____

_____

_____

_____

_____

_____

_____

_____

CAPTURE A MEMORY THAT WOULD OTHERWISE FADE AWAY...

WEATHER: _____   DATE: _____

THE HIKE

TRAIL NAME:
LENGTH OF TRAIL, LEVEL OF DIFFICULTY, AVERAGE HIKING TIME:

FEATURES OF THE HIKE:
HIKING PARTNERS, ELEVATION CHANGES, WATER AVAILABILITY
(WATER CACHE AREAS) :

MOMENTS OF REFLECTION:
WHAT I MOST WANT TO REMEMBER ABOUT THIS HIKE, SCENIC
VIEWPOINTS:

_____

_____

_____

_____

_____

_____

_____

_____

_____

_____

_____

_____

_____

_____

_____

TAKE A DEEP BREATH, TILT YOUR HEAD BACK— WRITE WHAT'S ON YOUR MIND...

DATE:

_____

_____

_____

_____

_____

_____

_____

_____

_____

_____

_____

_____

_____

_____

_____

_____

_____

_____

_____

CAPTURE A MEMORY THAT WOULD OTHERWISE FADE AWAY...

WEATHER: _____   DATE: _____

THE HIKE

TRAIL NAME:
LENGTH OF TRAIL, LEVEL OF DIFFICULTY, AVERAGE HIKING TIME:

FEATURES OF THE HIKE:
HIKING PARTNERS, ELEVATION CHANGES, WATER AVAILABILITY (WATER CACHE AREAS) :

MOMENTS OF REFLECTION:
WHAT I MOST WANT TO REMEMBER ABOUT THIS HIKE, SCENIC VIEWPOINTS:

DATE:

_____

_____

_____

_____

_____

_____

_____

_____

_____

_____

_____

_____

_____

_____

TAKE A DEEP BREATH, TILT YOUR HEAD BACK— WRITE WHAT'S ON YOUR
MIND...

DATE:

_____

_____

_____

_____

_____

_____

_____

_____

_____

_____

_____

_____

_____

_____

_____

_____

CAPTURE A MEMORY THAT WOULD OTHERWISE FADE AWAY...

THE HIKE

TRAIL NAME:
LENGTH OF TRAIL, LEVEL OF DIFFICULTY, AVERAGE HIKING TIME:

FEATURES OF THE HIKE:
HIKING PARTNERS, ELEVATION CHANGES, WATER AVAILABILITY
(WATER CACHE AREAS) :

MOMENTS OF REFLECTION:
WHAT I MOST WANT TO REMEMBER ABOUT THIS HIKE, SCENIC
VIEWPOINTS:

_____

_____

_____

_____

_____

_____

_____

_____

_____

_____

_____

_____

_____

_____

_____

_____

_____

TAKE A DEEP BREATH, TILT YOUR HEAD BACK— WRITE WHAT'S ON YOUR MIND...

DATE:

_____

_____

_____

_____

_____

_____

_____

_____

_____

_____

_____

_____

_____

_____

_____

_____

CAPTURE A MEMORY THAT WOULD OTHERWISE FADE AWAY...

WEATHER: _____   DATE: _____

THE HIKE

TRAIL NAME:
LENGTH OF TRAIL, LEVEL OF DIFFICULTY, AVERAGE HIKING TIME:

FEATURES OF THE HIKE:
HIKING PARTNERS, ELEVATION CHANGES, WATER AVAILABILITY
(WATER CACHE AREAS) :

MOMENTS OF REFLECTION:
WHAT I MOST WANT TO REMEMBER ABOUT THIS HIKE, SCENIC
VIEWPOINTS:

_____

_____

_____

_____

_____

_____

_____

_____

_____

_____

_____

_____

_____

_____

TAKE A DEEP BREATH, TILT YOUR HEAD BACK— WRITE WHAT'S ON YOUR MIND...

DATE:

_____

_____

_____

_____

_____

_____

_____

_____

_____

_____

_____

_____

_____

_____

_____

_____

_____

CAPTURE A MEMORY THAT WOULD OTHERWISE FADE AWAY...

WEATHER: _____   DATE: _____

THE HIKE

TRAIL NAME:
LENGTH OF TRAIL, LEVEL OF DIFFICULTY, AVERAGE HIKING TIME:

FEATURES OF THE HIKE:
HIKING PARTNERS, ELEVATION CHANGES, WATER AVAILABILITY
(WATER CACHE AREAS) :

MOMENTS OF REFLECTION:
WHAT I MOST WANT TO REMEMBER ABOUT THIS HIKE, SCENIC
VIEWPOINTS:

DATE:

_____

_____

_____

_____

_____

_____

_____

_____

_____

_____

_____

_____

_____

_____

TAKE A DEEP BREATH, TILT YOUR HEAD BACK— WRITE WHAT'S ON YOUR
MIND...

DATE:

_____

_____

_____

_____

_____

_____

_____

_____

_____

_____

_____

_____

_____

_____

_____

_____

_____

_____

CAPTURE A MEMORY THAT WOULD OTHERWISE FADE AWAY...

THE HIKE

TRAIL NAME:
LENGTH OF TRAIL, LEVEL OF DIFFICULTY, AVERAGE HIKING TIME:

FEATURES OF THE HIKE:
HIKING PARTNERS, ELEVATION CHANGES, WATER AVAILABILITY
(WATER CACHE AREAS) :

MOMENTS OF REFLECTION:
WHAT I MOST WANT TO REMEMBER ABOUT THIS HIKE, SCENIC
VIEWPOINTS:

_____

_____

_____

_____

_____

_____

_____

_____

_____

_____

_____

_____

_____

TAKE A DEEP BREATH, TILT YOUR HEAD BACK— WRITE WHAT'S ON YOUR MIND...

DATE:

CAPTURE A MEMORY THAT WOULD OTHERWISE FADE AWAY...

THE HIKE

TRAIL NAME:
LENGTH OF TRAIL, LEVEL OF DIFFICULTY, AVERAGE HIKING TIME:

FEATURES OF THE HIKE:
HIKING PARTNERS, ELEVATION CHANGES, WATER AVAILABILITY (WATER CACHE AREAS) :

MOMENTS OF REFLECTION:
WHAT I MOST WANT TO REMEMBER ABOUT THIS HIKE, SCENIC VIEWPOINTS:

_____

_____

_____

_____

_____

_____

_____

_____

_____

_____

_____

_____

_____

_____

TAKE A DEEP BREATH, TILT YOUR HEAD BACK— WRITE WHAT'S ON YOUR MIND...

DATE:

_____

_____

_____

_____

_____

_____

_____

_____

_____

_____

_____

_____

_____

_____

_____

_____

CAPTURE A MEMORY THAT WOULD OTHERWISE FADE AWAY...

WEATHER: _____   DATE: _____

THE HIKE

TRAIL NAME:
LENGTH OF TRAIL, LEVEL OF DIFFICULTY, AVERAGE HIKING TIME:

FEATURES OF THE HIKE:
HIKING PARTNERS, ELEVATION CHANGES, WATER AVAILABILITY (WATER CACHE AREAS) :

MOMENTS OF REFLECTION:
WHAT I MOST WANT TO REMEMBER ABOUT THIS HIKE, SCENIC VIEWPOINTS:

_____

_____

_____

_____

_____

_____

_____

_____

_____

_____

_____

_____

_____

_____

TAKE A DEEP BREATH, TILT YOUR HEAD BACK— WRITE WHAT'S ON YOUR MIND...

DATE:

_____

_____

_____

_____

_____

_____

_____

_____

_____

_____

_____

_____

_____

_____

_____

_____

_____

CAPTURE A MEMORY THAT WOULD OTHERWISE FADE AWAY...

THE HIKE

TRAIL NAME:
LENGTH OF TRAIL, LEVEL OF DIFFICULTY, AVERAGE HIKING TIME:

FEATURES OF THE HIKE:
HIKING PARTNERS, ELEVATION CHANGES, WATER AVAILABILITY
(WATER CACHE AREAS) :

MOMENTS OF REFLECTION:
WHAT I MOST WANT TO REMEMBER ABOUT THIS HIKE, SCENIC
VIEWPOINTS:

DATE:

_____

_____

_____

_____

_____

_____

_____

_____

_____

_____

_____

_____

_____

TAKE A DEEP BREATH, TILT YOUR HEAD BACK— WRITE WHAT'S ON YOUR MIND...

DATE:

_____

_____

_____

_____

_____

_____

_____

_____

_____

_____

_____

_____

_____

_____

_____

CAPTURE A MEMORY THAT WOULD OTHERWISE FADE AWAY...

WEATHER: _____   DATE: _____

THE HIKE

TRAIL NAME:
LENGTH OF TRAIL, LEVEL OF DIFFICULTY, AVERAGE HIKING TIME:

FEATURES OF THE HIKE:
HIKING PARTNERS, ELEVATION CHANGES, WATER AVAILABILITY (WATER CACHE AREAS) :

MOMENTS OF REFLECTION:
WHAT I MOST WANT TO REMEMBER ABOUT THIS HIKE, SCENIC VIEWPOINTS:

TAKE A DEEP BREATH, TILT YOUR HEAD BACK— WRITE WHAT'S ON YOUR
MIND...

DATE:

_____

_____

_____

_____

_____

_____

_____

_____

_____

_____

_____

_____

_____

_____

_____

_____

_____

CAPTURE A MEMORY THAT WOULD OTHERWISE FADE AWAY...

WEATHER: _____   DATE: _____

THE HIKE

TRAIL NAME:
LENGTH OF TRAIL, LEVEL OF DIFFICULTY, AVERAGE HIKING TIME:

FEATURES OF THE HIKE:
HIKING PARTNERS, ELEVATION CHANGES, WATER AVAILABILITY (WATER CACHE AREAS) :

MOMENTS OF REFLECTION:
WHAT I MOST WANT TO REMEMBER ABOUT THIS HIKE, SCENIC VIEWPOINTS:

_____
_____
_____
_____
_____
_____
_____
_____
_____
_____
_____
_____
_____
_____

TAKE A DEEP BREATH, TILT YOUR HEAD BACK— WRITE WHAT'S ON YOUR MIND...

DATE:

_____

_____

_____

_____

_____

_____

_____

_____

_____

_____

_____

_____

_____

_____

_____

_____

_____

CAPTURE A MEMORY THAT WOULD OTHERWISE FADE AWAY...

THE HIKE

TRAIL NAME:
LENGTH OF TRAIL, LEVEL OF DIFFICULTY, AVERAGE HIKING TIME:

FEATURES OF THE HIKE:
HIKING PARTNERS, ELEVATION CHANGES, WATER AVAILABILITY
(WATER CACHE AREAS) :

MOMENTS OF REFLECTION:
WHAT I MOST WANT TO REMEMBER ABOUT THIS HIKE, SCENIC
VIEWPOINTS:

_____

_____

_____

_____

_____

_____

_____

_____

_____

_____

_____

_____

_____

_____

_____

_____

TAKE A DEEP BREATH, TILT YOUR HEAD BACK— WRITE WHAT'S ON YOUR
MIND...

DATE:

_____

_____
_____
_____
_____
_____
_____
_____
_____
_____
_____
_____
_____
_____
_____
_____
_____
_____

CAPTURE A MEMORY THAT WOULD OTHERWISE FADE AWAY...

"I HAVE AN INSANE CALLING TO BE WHERE I'M NOT"

GO, SEEK, DO

SECTION FIVE

FAQ
MAPS

WHAT GOES DOWN, MUST COME UP
EXPLORE THE GREAT GC - GRAND CANYON
HIKING JOURNAL

SECTION FIVE

FAQ
MAPS

FAQ

1. Do I need a permit to hike the GC?
If you want to day hike or take a horseback ride in the canyon, no permit is necessary. However all overnight trips must obtain a permit through the Backcountry Information Center at Grand Canyon National Park.

2. Do I need a reservation?
If you want to spend the night, camp or experience a once-in-a-lifetime experience of sleeping inside the canyon, Plan 1- 2 years in advance. See Section 3.

3. What is the optimal time to begin your hike?
The early bird gets the worm.

4. What to pack in your backpack?
See Section 2 Pages 25-29
Checklist: The Essentials for your Day Hike

5. How much water should you bring?
See section 2 Pages 25-29 Checklist: The Essentials for your Day Hike

6. What should you wear for hiking?
See Section 2 Pages 25-29
, Checklist: The Essentials for your Day Hike

7. Is there any mobile network available?

VERIZON ACTUALLY HAS A TOWER IN THE GRAND CANYON PARK. THEIR CUSTOMERS GET THE BEST RECEPTION, BUT REMEMBER YOU ARE DEEP IN A CANYON.

8. Where is the best place to park?

PARK AT THE GRAND CANYON VISITOR CENTER. THERE IS ALSO A FREE SHUTTLE BUS TO TAKE YOU AROUND THE VILLAGE. SAVE FUEL, AND SAVE THE ENVIRONMENT, NO TICKETS REQUIRED.

9. Where should I stay?

SEE SECTION THREE: WHERE TO SLEEP.

10. Best season/month to go?

WINTER, SPRING, SUMMER, AND FALL.

11. Where do I fly into?

THERE ARE SEVERAL OPTIONS:

PHOENIX SKY HARBOR IS THE CLOSET INTERNATIONAL AIRPORT. LAND ON THE GROUND AND IN LESS THAN FOUR HOURS YOU WILL BE AT THE SOUTH RIM. FLY INTO THE SMALL AIRPORT OF FLAGSTAFF TO BE 92 MILES AWAY. LAS VEGAS INTERNATIONAL AIRPORT IS CLOSEST TO THE WEST RIM AND ABOUT 5 HOURS TO THE SOUTH RIM. THERE'S ALSO A SMALL AIRPORT IN KINGMAN, PRESCOTT AND SEDONA.

12. **Where is Havasupai?**

THE HAVASUPAI INDIAN RESERVATION IS A NATIVE AMERICAN RESERVATION FOR THE HAVASUPAI PEOPLE, SURROUNDED ENTIRELY BY THE GRAND CANYON NATIONAL PARK. THEIR TRIBE HAS LIVED IN THE GRAND CANYON FOR OVER 800 YEARS. MUCH OF THEIR RESERVATION WAS TAKEN AND WAS PART OF THE GRAND CANYON NATIONAL PARK BUT IN 1975, 188,000 ACRES WAS RETURNED TO THE HAVASUPAI. HAVASUPAI IS HOME TO THE PEOPLE OF THE BLUE GREEN WATER. TO BUY A HIKING JOURNAL SPECIFICALLY FOR HAVASUPAI GO TO AMAZON.COM/AUTHOR/BOOKSWITHSOUL. HAVASUPAI HIKING JOURNAL: THE KEEPERS OF THE GRAND CANYON.

13. **Where is the skywalk?**

THE SKY WALK IS LOCATED ON THE HUALAPAI INDIAN RESERVATION THAT IS JUST EAST OF LAS VEGAS, KNOWN AS GRAND CANYON WEST. LOCATED ON THE WEST RIM OF THE GRAND CANYON, IT IS ONLY 3 HOUR DRIVE FROM VEGAS. IF YOU DARE WALK OUT ON A PIECE OF GLASS WITH 2000 FEET OF CANYON BELOW YOU, AND 3 MILES OF AIR IN FRONT OF YOU.

14. **Where is the best Place to see the Colorado river at the south rim?** GRANDVIEW POINT AND BRIGHT ANGEL TRAIL TO PLATEAU POINT.

15. **Are Pets allowed at the Grand Canyon?** PETS ARE NOT ALLOWED BELOW THE RIM, IN BUILDINGS OR ON SHUTTLE BUSES. LEASHED PETS ARE ALLOWED ON RIM AND GREENWAY TRAILS ONLY.

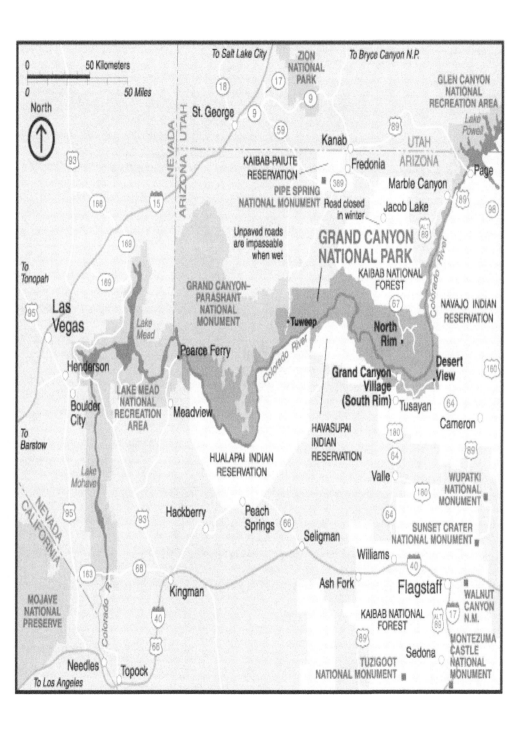

Getting Around the South Rim

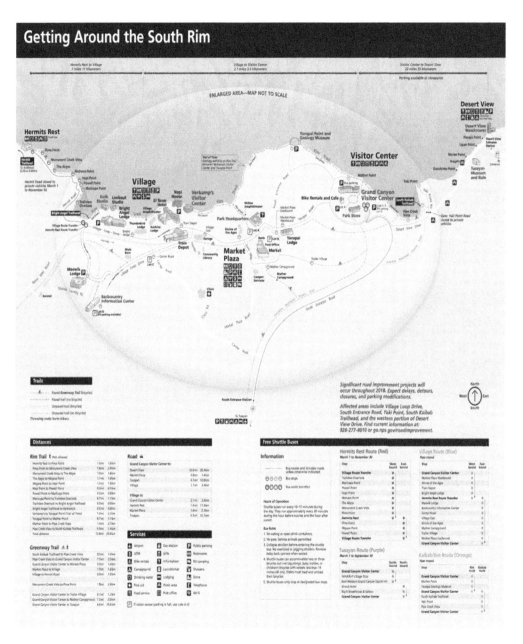

THIS MAP IS PART OF THE NATIONAL PARK SERVICES.
THE POCKET MAP IS PUBLISHED BY GRAND CANYON NATIONAL PARK WITH SUPPORT FROM
YOUR ENTRANCE FEES. IT IS AVAILABLE IN FRENCH, GERMAN, SPANISH, ITALIAN, JAPANESE,
CHINESE, AND KOREAN. AN ACCESSIBILITY GUIDE IS ALSO AVAILABLE. ASK IN VISITOR CENTERS
FOR A HIKING BROCHURE.

"BE INSPIRED FOR YOUR NEXT ADVENTURE."

A note about the Author:

Lisa Jewel Rafferty has hiked the Grand Canyon
countless times.
She states, "It is my favorite place in the whole world".
She has hiked a variety of trails including Hermit Trail to Dripping
Springs Day Hike, South Kaibab/Tonto/Bright Angel Day Hike,
Havasupai and she completed a rim to rim hike with her
hiking friend Nancy Culver. She only started hiking the canyon in
2014 and encourages everyone to make a plan and hike one of the
most amazing locations on earth.
She encourages folks to record their Hiking Memories.
Her favorite moment of hiking the GC: taking a nap on the park
bench at Indian gardens . 😎

Lisa is an executive at Aon and spends
her free time with her family, traveling and blazing trails all over
the world.

Anita Kaltenbaugh & Books with Soul® is honored to partner with
Lisa and help others preserve their experience of the
magnificent Grand Canyon. Check out bookswithsoul.com

This book provides information to both novice and experienced
hikers and serves as a guide and journal to one of the world most
precious treasures.
Experience the wonder of the grand canyon National Park
Celebrating 100 years in 2019